DIFFUSING
ESSENTIAL OILS

For Beginners

Patti Roberts

Cover designed by Paradox Book Covers & Formatting

WitchWood ESTATE COLLECTABLES

DIFFUSING ESSENTIAL OILS

COMPILED BY
PATTI ROBERTS

Review and recommendation.

Since doing my certificate in Clinical Aromatherapy in the early 2000s, I must have read dozens of aromatherapy books, ranging from heavy texts for the professional practitioner to introductory ones for the layman. But I don't think I've seen a better resource for the lay user than this one.

T. Ormiston-smith.

Freebies – ebooks only.
Once Were Friends.
The Witches' Journal.
A collection of recipes, poetry, Witches' panty, reading tealeaves, broom history, familiars, candles, flowers, herbs and more.
Diffusing Essential Oils.
Writing Tips From Authors.
Believe.

Witchwood Estate
Witchwood Estate – Going Home – (book 1) FREE
Witchwood Estate – Ferntree Falls
Witchwood Estate – Print Edition (book 1 and 2)
Witchwood Estate – Cursed (book 3)
Witchwood Estate – Timeless (book 4)
Witchwood Estate – Witches Bitches (book 5)

Witchwood Estate Spinoff
Tales from Witchwood - Charmed by Witches

Witchwood Estate Collectables
The Witches' Journal
Diffusing Essential Oils
Mother Nature's Medicine Cabinet
Little Book Of Smoothies

Paradox Series
Paradox – The Angels Are Here (book 1) 2010 FREE
Paradox – Progeny Of Innocence (book 2)
Paradox – Bound By Blood (book 3)
Paradox – Equilibrium (book 4)
Paradox – Elemental (book 5)

Standalone Novel
About Three Authors – Whoever Said Love Was Easy?

Non-fiction
Surviving Tracy – true stories from the survivors of Cyclone Tracy.

Disclaimer.

The content in this book is not intended to be a substitute for professional medical advice, diagnosis, or treatment in any way. Always seek the advice of your physician or a qualified health provider with any questions you have regarding your specific situation. Any statements or claims within this book about the possible health benefits using essential oils have not been evaluated by any Food or Drug Administration. The information in this book is not intended to diagnose, treat, cure or prevent any disease.

Warning.

It is advised to always keep essential oils out of reach from small children and animals. Some oils can also be problematic for those with asthma and allergies, so don't go overboard! Very high dosages of some essential oils can irritate the membranes which can lead to headaches and dizziness. Essential oils can enter the body in three ways — applied directly to the skin, inhaled, or ingested. Check with your preferred health food store; they usually have an essential oil specialist on hand. Essential oils should never be directly burned, when doing so, the chemical structure is dramatically changed and can become toxic. It is also stressed that some oils should never be used on babies or young children. Your pets should also be taken into consideration when using some essential oils.

Dilution is significantly important when using ALL ESSENTIAL OILS. There is no exception to this rule. No matter what brand you buy, what essential oil you are using, or how much, it is not safe to use ANY essential oil neat without diluting it in a carrier oil or some other form of dilution - such as water.

How Many Drops of Essential Oils Should I Put in My Diffuser?

Diffuser Size	Number of Drops
100ml	3-5
200ml	6-10
300ml	9-12
400ml	12-15
500ml	15-20

CONTENTS

A Note From The Author.

There are many diffusers available on the market, and I recommend you shop around and do some research before you purchase one that you'll be happy with.

I love using my diffuser and use them (I have 3) on a daily basis. Not only for the lovely aromas but the bonus health benefits as well.

Not so long ago I used plug-in air fresheners to keep my home and office smelling nice but having learned of the toxic chemicals used in these products, I have opted for the healthier and friendlier option using essential oils.

Of course, there are many ways for using essential oils to benefit your health and wellbeing, however, this book is focused on using some of these remarkable oils in diffusers.

Patti.

PATTI ROBERTS

Why diffuse essential oils? Because diffusing distributes essential oil molecules into the air so perfectly, it is an effective way in which to maximize the beneficial properties of essential oils.

ESSENTIAL OILS - DIFFUSING BENEFITS.

A diffuser is a household must-have that can replace plug-in air fresheners to make your home smell nice. Air fresheners contain nasty chemical ingredients linked to numerous health issues. When you see the term 'fragrance' on an air freshener, it can include hundreds of toxic chemicals referred to as 'fragrance'.

If you have pets or small children living with you in the home, burning candles or incense can be hazardous. With your essential oil diffuser, you can reap the benefits of aromatherapy, and to a much greater effect, without the risk of burns, wax spills, and other life-threatening accidents.

The term 'Diffusing' means to take a liquid and then vaporize it so that it can be inhaled and absorbed through the lungs. You receive the benefits of the oils simply by breathing as you normally would while you get on with your day. It's a simple practice, yet the benefits of using essential oils are enormous to your health and well-being. Essential oils not only influence your moods and increase focus and concentration, but they also support your family's immune system.

If you're a little bit witchy, then you are no stranger to natural living practices, and you no doubt already know a thing or two about using essential oil in diffusers to improve your health, increase your energy, and to help you sleep better. Not to mention de-stress and put you in a better mood – and who doesn't need that from time to time? I know I do. Diffusers are great for all those benefits and more. Sharing is caring, so keep one in the office to help you and your coworkers stay balanced and refreshed throughout the day. Always check with others, however. Some may not like your preferences in particular oil blends – pregnant women, for example, or those with certain allergies.

In addition to affecting our moods, inhaling essential oils can have many other benefits. Essential oils cross into the bloodstream via our lungs, quickly delivering essential oils to the whole body. Additionally, inhaling essential oils can help reduce the discomfort of respiratory infections like colds, flu and sinus congestion.

ADD THESE SIX OILS TO YOUR NATURAL MEDICINE CABINET.

Lavender: One of the most commonly used oils, lavender helps with relaxation and sleep, lowers anxiety, improves mood, and heals burns, cuts, rashes, stings. Restores skin complexion and reduces acne. Slows aging with powerful antioxidants. Improves eczema and psoriasis.

Frankincense: Boosts your immune system, reduces inflammation, heals age spots, supports brain function. Anti-inflammatory, heal bruising, reduce scars, boost emotional well-being. Research shows that it may also be helpful in fighting cancer.

Lemon: Perfect to use in homemade cleaning products. It improves lymph drainage and cleanses the body. Nourishes the skin and promotes weight loss. Calms stomach and relieves nausea. Helps people overcome addictions and improves mood to fight depression.

Peppermint: Supports digestion, improves focus, boosts energy, reduces fever, soothes headaches, and relieves muscle and joint pain. Clear sinuses, improve asthma and bronchitis. Aids weight loss by suppressing cravings.
Tea tree oil: (Melaleuca): Is a natural anti-bacterial, anti-fungal, reduces bad odors and helps stimulate the immune system. Prevents and reduces infection and cleans the air of pathogens and allergens.

Orange: Antispasmodic. Relaxes muscular and nervous spasms and coughing. Alleviates anxiety, anger, depression, and inflammation. Aphrodisiac properties. Orange aids both septic, fungal infections, and tetanus as they inhibit microbial growth and disinfect the wounds. Ideal for people who suffer from depression or chronic anxiety. Helps eliminate houseflies.

Some of my favorite essential oils.

Clary Sage.
Eucalyptus.
Frankincense.
Lavender.
Myrrh.
Orange.
Oregano.
Wild oregano
Peppermint.
Tea Tree.
Vetiver.

My list grows by the day!

BLENDS OF ESSENTIAL OILS TO TRY IN YOUR DIFFUSER.

For those who have yet to invest in a Diffuser, the reasons to do so is as long as a nine cat's tails and then some, here are some examples of how you could use one at home or workplace.

In this ebook, you will find some suggestions for the uses of essential oil blends in your diffuser. Keep in mind, however, that you can always tweak the ingredients to suit your preferences. Okay, let's get started.

RELAXATION AND SLEEP – OPTION 1.

Everyone needs a good night's sleep – eight hours is the recommendation for optimal health benefits. Did you know that if you don't get enough sleep, it can be harder to maintain a healthy weight? One of the best uses for essential oils is their ability to help you unwind at the end of the day. While there are other methods for using essential oils to work their magic, the diffuser is by far the easiest of them all. Set up a diffuser on your bedside table to help your mind and body unwind, optimizing a better night's sleep.

Recommended oils:
2 drops Chamomile.
2 drops Lavender.
2 drops Clary Sage.

RELAXATION AND SLEEP – OPTION 2.

Diffuse for a restful night's sleep, especially for mental chatter. Soothes the systems while supporting a healthier immune system.

Ingredients:
2 drops Lavender.
2 drops Vetiver.
2 drops Roman Chamomile.

IMMUNITY BOOST BLEND.

This blend is best for boosting your immune system. It also promotes healthy cell function. Not only that, it's ideal for cleansing the air and uplifting your mood.

Ingredients:
2 drops Lemon.
2 drops Melaleuca (tea tree oil).
1 drops Clove.
1 drops Frankincense.

BANISH ILLNESS.

Using a diffuser in your home - or office - is a great way to keep cold, flu, and other nasties at bay. Many essential oils are powerful anti-microbial, so when they're introduced into the air in vapor form, the organic compounds in oils come into direct contact with airborne pathogens before they can invade your body. Essential oils can also boost your immune system. Diffusers also aid in keeping your airways moist and healthy, so you are better prepared for any microbes that do make their way into your body.

Recommended oils:
2 drops Tea tree oil.
2 drops Sage.
2 drops Rosemary.
2 drops Orange.
2 drops Frankincense.
2 drops Thyme.
2 drops of Myrrh.

Add your own blend here.

BREATHE EASY - 1.

Essential oils are perfect for reducing inflammation and congestion, helping you breathe more easily. If you are prone to allergies or other breathing disorders, try diffusing essential oils where you spend a majority of your time.

Recommended oils:
2 drops Peppermint.
2 drops Rosemary.
2 drops Lemon.
2 drops Eucalyptus
2 drops Frankincense.

BREATHE EASY - 2.

Ingredients:
4 drops Frankincense.
3 drops Lavender.
6 drops Clary Sage.

HEADACHE RELIEF.

While Peppermint is a great way for relieving headaches when applied to the temples and back of the neck – Clary Sage for hormonal headaches – you can also diffuse a blend that will help bring continued relief to headaches.

NOTE: Don't forget to drink plenty of water to hydrate yourself throughout the day.

Ingredients:
2 drops Marjoram.
2 drops Thyme.
2 drops Rosemary.
2 drops Peppermint.
2 drops Lavender.

Many of the above blends can also be added to water in spray bottles to use around the home and office.

NOTES

MOOD ELEVATING.

Just as a diffuser can help you to de-stress after a long day, they can also be used to create a positive and energizing mood. This blend is wonderful for when your witchy mojo isn't firing on all cylinders, and you're feeling a little sad or depressed. You can use your diffuser to inspiration, and to set a positive atmosphere during business meetings and social gatherings.

Is there romance in the air? Create a romantic atmosphere and see where the evening takes you.

Recommended oils:
2 drops Orange.
2 drops Jasmine.
2 drops Rose.
2 drops Vetiver.
2 drops ylang ylang.
2 drops Sandalwood.
2 drops Vanilla.

UPLIFTING.

Ingredients:
3 drops Bergamot.
2 drops Geranium.
1 drop Orange.
1 drop Rose.
1 drop Vetiver.

BE HAPPY.

Adding these oils together will put you in a happy mood - Ideal for when you have friends coming over for a visit.

Ingredients:
3 drops Bergamot.
2 drops Geranium.
3 drops Lavender.
1 drop Vetiver.

STRESS AND ANXIETY - 1.

Diffuse these oils to alleviate the tension caused by feelings of stress and anxiety.

Ingredients:
2 drops Lavender.
2 drops Frankincense.
1 drop Orange.
1 drop Vetiver.

STRESS AND ANXIETY - 2.

Ingredients:
4 drops Cedarwood.
3 drops Bergamot.
2 drops Jasmine.
1 drop Vetiver.

STRESS AND ANXIETY - 3.

Ingredients:
5 drops Sandalwood.
1 drop Vetiver.
1 drop Roman Chamomile.
1 drop Lavender.
1 drop Orange.

CALMING BLEND.

About to lose your witchy Mojo? Dive into this one quick! You can also add it to a spray bottle for a quick spritz when you need it.

Ingredients:
4 drops Lavender.
3 drops Geranium.
2 drops Roman Chamomile.

2 drops Clary Sage.
2 drops Ylang Ylang.
1 drop Frankincense.

HYPO KIDS.

Do your kids need help calming down? Yes? Then try this combination of oils in the diffuser when you want to help them settle naturally.

Ingredients:
2 drops Lavender.
2 drops Roman Chamomile.
2 drops Vetiver.

AFTER SCHOOL - PEACE & CALMING.

Ingredients:

3 drops Orange.

3 drops Patchouli.

2 drops Lavender.

COLOR ME:

RISE AND SHINE SLEEPYHEAD.

If you're so not a morning person, like me, diffusing essential oils will help you start your morning in a better frame of mind. This blend will awaken your senses and lift your mood as well as calming you in the process.

Ingredients:
2 drops Peppermint or Spearmint oil.
2 drops Orange.
1 drop Ylang Ylang.

SUNSHINE AND BUTTERFLIES BLEND.

Ingredients:
5 drops Orange Essential Oil.
5 drops Grapefruit Essential Oil.
2 drops Lime Essential Oil.

EXTRA BOOST BLEND.

Ingredients:
5 drops Rosemary.
5 drops Grapefruit.
5 drops Lime.

BALANCING BLEND.

Ingredients:
3 drops Neroli.
3 drops Orange.
1 drop Frankincense.
1 drop Lemon.
1 drop Ylang Ylang.

IMPROVE MEMORY.

Using oils in your diffuser is a highly-effective way to super-charge your brainiac cells. Many essential oils have adaptogenic qualities – meaning that they are soothing when you're stressed to the max, but they can also give you a quick pick-me-up when you're feeling lethargic. The oils in the air will balance your mood and help you to focus better.

Recommended oils:
2 drops Peppermint.
2 drops Eucalyptus.
2 drops Lemon.
2 drops Orange.
2 drops Rosemary.

TIME TO STUDY.

Try these blends when it's time to focus for an exam or an assignment. When studying for anything that needs your concentration, it's a good idea to diffuse an oil or blend – taking a scented handkerchief with you may help also. Inhaling the same aromas while taking the exam has been said to help with memory recall.

Ingredients:
1 drop Basil.
2 drops Lemon.
3 drops Rosemary.

OR

2 drops Peppermint.
2 drops Grapefruit.
2 drops Rosemary.

OR
1 drop Basil.
1 drop Rosemary.
1 drop Orange.
2 drops Grapefruit.

NOTES

KICK BUTT WORKOUT BLEND.

Time for a workout!

Ingredients:
2 drops Lemon.
2 drops Peppermint.
2 drops Grapefruit.

KITCHEN RULES.

This is a great blend to diffuse in the kitchen while you're cooking.

Ingredients:
3 drops Rosemary.
3 drops Lemon.

STINKY.

Whether it's a musty closet or a stinky fish smell in the trashcan, this combination works well to illuminate unpleasant odors.

Ingredients:
3 drops Lemongrass.
3 drops Orange.
1 drop Oregano.
3 drops Peppermint.

REPEL INSECTS.

Whether your problem is with mosquitoes, house flies, fruit flies or moths, you can use essential oils in your diffuser to deter these pesky bugs from taking up residence in your home. I have a lot of fruit at home, so I'm always having a problem with fruit flies.

Recommended oils

2 drops Clove.

2 drops Lemongrass.

2 drops Rosemary.

2 drops Cedarwood.

BROKEN HEARTED?

Strengthen your emotions with this blend.

Ingredients:
2 drops Frankincense.
2 drops Orange.
2 drops Bergamot.
2 drops Clary Sage.

SEXY TIME BLEND – 1.

Ingredients:
1 drops Ginger.
1 drop Lime.
1 drop Ylang Ylang.
5 drops Sandalwood.
3 drops Bergamot.

SEXY TIME BLEND – 2.

Ingredients:
1 drop Orange.
1 drop Sandalwood.
1 drop Ylang Ylang.
2 drops Cinnamon.
2 drops Patchouli.

Add your own sexy blends.

SAY BYE BYE TO ALLERGIES.

Ingredients:
3 drops Peppermint.
3 drops Lemon.
3 drops Lavender.

Diffusing essential oils like tea tree, lemon, eucalyptus, lavender and peppermint oil can help to open up nasal passages, improve circulation, and sooth irritations. Essential oils also have antimicrobial properties that help to fight infections, bacteria, parasites, microorganisms and other toxins that can trigger allergic reactions. By diffusing essential oils throughout your home will leave the air in your home disinfected, clean and refreshingly clear.

Essential oils can be used as an alternative or complementary treatment for your allergy symptoms. Derived from plants, they can be used in a variety of ways. Popular ways for you to use essential oils include:

- diffusing them into the air
- using them in bath and spa products
- applying them to the skin when diluted
- spraying them into the air
- breathing them in directly from the container

ARE YOU EXPECTING?

Firstly, congratulations! You'll be very happy to know that there are lots of essential oils you can use safely during your pregnancy.

Bergamot.
Cedarwood.
Citronella* use with caution.
Clove* use with caution.
Copaiba.
Coriander.
Cypress.
Frankincense.
Geranium.
Grapefruit.
Lavender.
Lemon.
Lime.
Mandarin.

Melaleuca.
Neroli.
Orange.
Rosewood.
Patchouli.
Palmarosa.
Peppermint* use with caution.
Petitgrain.
Sandalwood.
Tangerine.
Vetiver.
Ylang Ylang.

Although Peppermint oil can assist with nausea in the early months, you should use it with caution. Peppermint oil can also help with, heartburn and other digestive upsets, however, because it is a strong oil, don't use it a lot or too often. One drop well-diluted or put in a diffuser is plenty. Using Peppermint oil past twenty-five weeks can reduce breast milk production in some women.

Lemon or Citrus Fresh oils diluted in a carrier oil and massaged into the bottom of your feet may also support the digestive problems you may be experiencing. So, put your feet up and let your partner spoil you with a much-deserved foot massage.

For fatigue, oils such as Lemon and Orange as well as a little Peppermint can be invigorating. You could diffuse these oils in the morning or mid-afternoon.

If you prefer, create a spritz spray filling a -4 oz (118 ml.) bottle of distilled water with witch hazel and 5 drops of Lemon.
Fatigued? The key is plenty of good quality sleep - 8 hours if possible. Drink plenty of fluids as dehydration can cause major fatigue, especially if you are nursing. Drink plenty of water, broths, teas, and coconut water to hydrate.

For sleep. With pregnancy, often comes restless sleep. Are you tired during the day, but can't sleep at night? There are some excellent oils for relaxation that can be used safely during pregnancy. The best oils to use to promote restful sleep include Lavender, Chamomile, Cedarwood, Vetiver, and Tangerine. You can diffuse any combination of these before bed. Or you can dilute oils with a carrier oil and apply to the bottom of your feet. You can even make up a sleep spritz with water and spray the mist on your sheets and pillow.

For headaches, Grapefruit or Ylang Ylang oils work very well. For support and ease, add 1 drop per 1 tsp. to a carrier oil and rub into the temples, and the back of your neck and inhale. You can also use Peppermint oil.

You can and should enjoy essential oils during your pregnancy, just don't overdo it, and if you have any concerns, ask your physician or natural health practitioner.

BABY NAME IDEAS

ESSENTIAL OILS - BABIES & CHILDREN.

Keep all essential oils out of reach of children. Certain essential oils are toxic if ingested, and no essential oils should be given orally to children.

Do not use essential oils on babies less than 3 months of age. Their skin is not mature enough. There should be even more caution taken with premature babies. Check with your medical professional before using essential oils on babies, particularly premature babies.

Essential oils safe for use, topically or diffusion, on babies 3+ months old.

The maximum recommended amount of essential oils to use on babies (3+ months) topically should not exceed 1 to 2 drops of essential oil per ounce of carrier oil.

Roman Chamomile.
Dill.
Lavender.
Yarrow, Blue.

Essential oils safe for use, topically or diffusion, on babies 6+ months.

The maximum recommended amount of essential oils to use on babies 6+ months topically should not exceed 3 to 5 drops of essential oil per ounce of carrier oil.

Carrot Seed.	Neroli.
Coriander.	Sandalwood.
Cypress.	Spruce.
Fir needle.	Sweet Orange.
Geranium.	Tangerine.
Grapefruit.	Tea Tree.
Mandarin.	

Essential oils safe for use, topically or diffusion, on children 2+ years.

The maximum recommended amount of essential oils to use on children 2+ years topically should never surpass 20 drops of essential oil per ounce of carrier oil.

Basil, Lemon.	Myrrh.
Basil, Sweet.	Sweet Marjoram.
Clary Sage.	Patchouli.
Frankincense.	Spearmint.
Juniper Berry.	Tea Tree, Lemon.
Lime.	Verbena, Lemon.
Melissa/Lemon Balm.	Vetiver. Valerian.

Essential oils safe for use, topically or diffusion, on children 6+ years.

The maximum recommended amount of essential oils to use on children 6+ years topically, should never surpass 30 drops of essential oil per ounce of carrier oil.

Fennel, sweet and bitter.
Laurel Leaf/Bay Laurel.
Marjoram, Spanish.
Niaouli.
Sage, Greek/White.

Essential oils safe for use, topically or diffusion, on children 10+ years of age.

By this age, most of the essential oils are safe for topical use or diffusion, though you should always be sure to introduce each oil slowly and individually just to make sure there are no adverse reactions or allergies.

*Peppermint, *eucalyptus, and *rosemary essential oils should all be avoided in younger children because they contain a chemical called 1,8-cineol and menthol.

PETS

If you use a diffuser, keep your pets out of the room when using the essential oils during your treatment period. If you wear certain essential oils on pulse points, be mindful when patting your pets. Essential oils are natural, but the wrong essential oil can cause a negative reaction in our pets. However, aromatherapy is just as beneficial to our pets if used correctly. Every pet is different and therefore may have different reactions to different essential oils. There are some essential oils that you will want to be careful about using when around your pets. Follow is a guide that can assist you in making informed choices.

Though there are essential oils that can cause your pets problems and should be avoided, there are plenty of essential oils that can be used to help them.

ESSENTIAL OILS THAT ARE IDEAL FOR PETS.

Though there are essential oils that can cause problems for your pets, there are plenty of essential oils that can be used to help them.

Use in moderation – and always check with your veterinarian when in doubt.

Cedarwood: Assists in repelling pests and also promotes healthy skin and coat.

Chamomile: Promotes relaxation and sleep, and also supports healthy digestion.

Carrot Seed: Supports healthy skin and assists as a topical treatment for dryness.

Clary Sage: Calming for nervousness and over excitability.

Geranium: Ideal for repelling pests naturally and as a treatment for common ear infections.

Lavender: Relieves anxiety, especially during times of prolonged separation or during long trips. Lavender oil, which is found in some cat litter and cat toys, is also generally safe when added to products designed for your cat. It is important to always check with a veterinarian, however, if you are thinking of using concentrated lavender oil for aromatherapy or some other purpose. The ingestion of lavender oil can be risky, so be sure to consult a reliable professional first! Sedative Properties: The University of Maryland report that lavender has been used with cats and dogs, as well as humans, as a calming agent or sedative. Again, though, be sure to seek advice from your vet about this use for lavender before purchasing new products, particularly if these products claim to be medicinal.

Marjoram: Repels pests and assists in treating skin infections and irritations.

Myrrh: Can help to fight allergies while promoting a healthy skin and coat.

**Peppermint: Soothes the pain from pets with arthritis and hip dysplasia. It also repels pests. **Some say yes to peppermint, some say no – check with your veterinarian.

Ginger: Also relieves pain from arthritis and hip dysplasia while supporting healthy digestion.

Those are just a few of the essential oils you can use on your pets. If you are interested in learning more, you can always talk to a holistic veterinarian for more suggestions.

SAFE USE OF ESSENTIAL OILS.

Whether you decide to use essential oils for your pet or just yourself, it's important you exercise safety when using these oils. Pets have a far stronger sense of smell than we do and smaller bodies, so the biggest mistake a pet owner can make is using too much essential oil. One of the best ways to avoid this mistake is by using a high-quality diffuser that enables you to control the amount of oil emitted. In a smaller room for example with little ventilation, use the low setting.

USE HIGH-QUALITY ESSENTIAL OILS.

Another important aspect of using essential oils around pets is to use a high-quality therapeutic grade oil. Lesser quality essential

oils are made with additives or diluted with carrier oils which may trigger sensitivities in your pet. They might also be a blend of oils which include other botanicals or absolutes that resemble the high-quality brands but potentially contain solvents that could be unhealthy for you and your fur baby. However, as long as you use the recommended essential oils, avoiding the oils that may trigger issues in your pets, they are perfectly safe. Since every pet is different, an essential oil that can benefit one might trigger a different response in another, so be aware.

CONSULT YOUR VETERINARIAN.

When it comes to our pets and essential oils, it is recommended that you consult with your preferred veterinarian for advice on the best way to use essential oils, particularly based on the pet's species, age, size and health history.

Research shows that essential oils can be quite safe for our dogs and cats and even very effective, but only when the correct amount is diluted and used correctly.

Using undiluted essential oil on yourself or your pets is always a mistake.

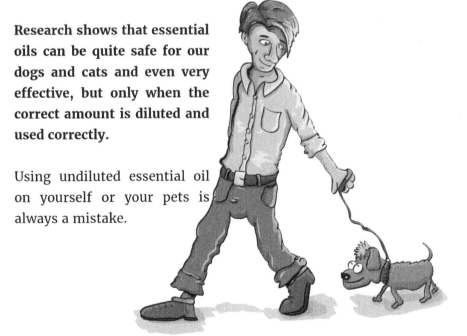

Unlike dogs, people, and horses, cats lack a liver enzyme (glucuronyl tranferase) required to break down the components of most essential oils.

KITTY.

If you have cats, you also need to be aware of certain oils. Cats, for example, are sensitive to essential oils containing polyphenolic compounds which interfere with their liver detoxification processes.

USE EXTRA CAUTION WHEN USING THE FOLLOWING ESSENTIALS OILS:

Cinnamon.

Tea tree.

Thyme.

Birch.

Wintergreen.

Clove.

Oregano.

Lemon Oil

Melaleuca Oil

**Peppermint – some say yes, some say no – check with your veterinarian.

POOCH

Use extra caution when using the following essentials oils:

Anise.
Clove
Garlic.
Horseradish.
Juniper.
Thyme.
Wintergreen.
Yarrow.

Do not add essential oils to your pet's food or drinking water.

Avoid using essential oils with puppies under ten weeks of age.

HERBS FOR FLU

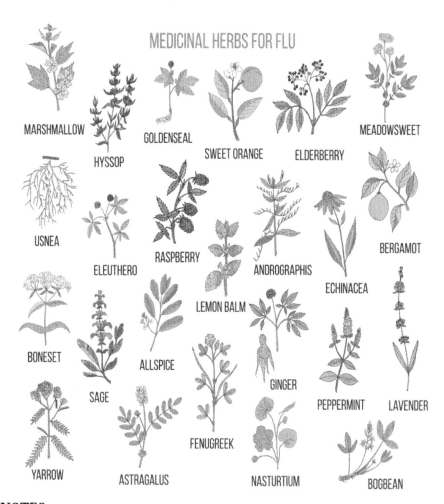

MEDICINAL HERBS FOR FLU

MARSHMALLOW

HYSSOP

GOLDENSEAL

SWEET ORANGE

ELDERBERRY

MEADOWSWEET

USNEA

ELEUTHERO

RASPBERRY

ANDROGRAPHIS

ECHINACEA

BERGAMOT

BONESET

SAGE

ALLSPICE

LEMON BALM

GINGER

PEPPERMINT

LAVENDER

YARROW

ASTRAGALUS

FENUGREEK

NASTURTIUM

BOGBEAN

NOTES

HERBS FOR DEPRESSION

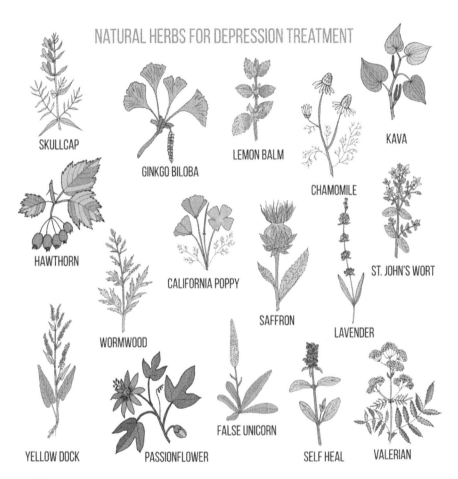

NATURAL HERBS FOR DEPRESSION TREATMENT

SKULLCAP

GINKGO BILOBA

LEMON BALM

CHAMOMILE

KAVA

HAWTHORN

CALIFORNIA POPPY

SAFFRON

ST. JOHN'S WORT

LAVENDER

WORMWOOD

YELLOW DOCK

PASSIONFLOWER

FALSE UNICORN

SELF HEAL

VALERIAN

NOTES

HERBS FOR ADD

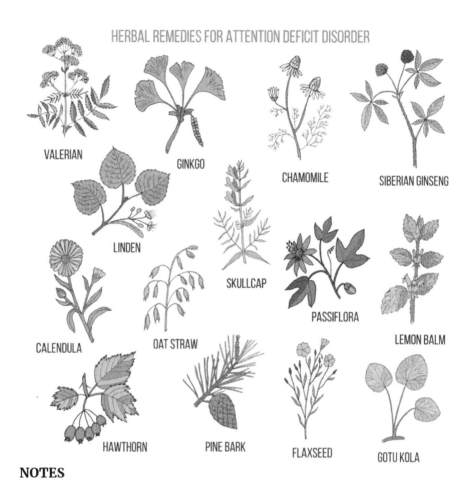

HERBAL REMEDIES FOR ATTENTION DEFICIT DISORDER

VALERIAN

GINKGO

CHAMOMILE

SIBERIAN GINSENG

LINDEN

SKULLCAP

PASSIFLORA

LEMON BALM

CALENDULA

OAT STRAW

HAWTHORN

PINE BARK

FLAXSEED

GOTU KOLA

NOTES

HERBS FOR ANTI AGING

NOTES

HERBS FOR COMMON COLD

BEST HERBS FOR THE COMMON COLD

BLACKBERRY

MILKVETCH

BONESET

ALLSPICE

AMUR CORK TREE

SCHIZANDRA

HEATHER

INULA

RASPBERRY

GINSENG

ECHINACEA

BROOKLIME

SCULLCAP

BLACK ELDER

GARLIC

LAVENDER

NOTES

ANTIMICROBIAL HERBS

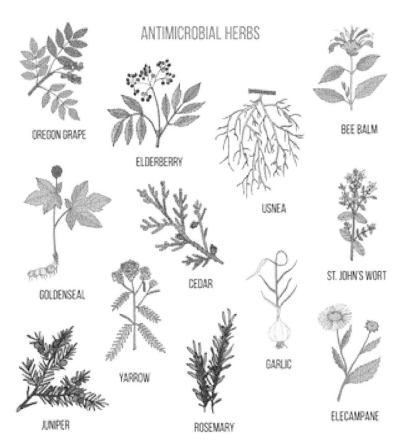

NOTES

HERBS FOR HAIR GROWTH

NOTES

HERBS FOR THE IMMUNE SYSTEM

NOTES

HERBS FOR PSORIASIS

NATURAL HERBS FOR PSORIASIS TREATMENT

OREGON GRAPE

BARBERRY

NEEM

RED CLOVER

OREGANO

BERGAMOT

KUTKI

CALENDULA

CAT'S CLAW

PAU D'ARCO

TEA TREE OIL

MILK THISTLE

CHICKWEED

ARNICA MONTANA

JUNIPER

BLACK WALNUT

CAYENNE

ALOE VERA

TURMERIC

NOTES

Mother Nature's Medicine Cabinet.

In ancient times, the plant kingdom provided our earliest ancestors with the natural healing powers derived from nature. Extracts and essences from plants and flowers were prized for their medicinal, spiritual, aromatic, and therapeutic value, including beauty benefits.

Aromatic plants, essences, and oils have traditionally been used during religious ceremonies and observances, beauty care and perfumes, food enhancement, and preservation. Aromatic plants were the basis for herbal and botanical medicines and remedies for thousands of years – they still are. In fact, they're the root of today's modern pharmaceuticals.

And as lifestyles rapidly changed to meet everyday challenges, and technology progressed in leaps and bounds, herbal knowledge soon fell by the wayside.

During the past century, as the side effects of many chemically based drugs come to light – not to mention the exuberant costs, natural healing has come full circle and has gradually found its way back into our homes. The Western World is standing up and taking notice. People are educating themselves about the wonderful uses and benefits of using essential oils, herbs, and spices. Mother nature's medicine cabinet is back, invoking endless remedies and in some cases, cures – without the side effects.

Granted. Natural healing may not replace the family doctor or chemically manufactured drugs entirely, but it certainly is a healthy alternative to consider when thinking about your health, beauty, wellbeing, and fitness regime.

Sample From Mother Natures Medicine Cabinet.

CANNABIS

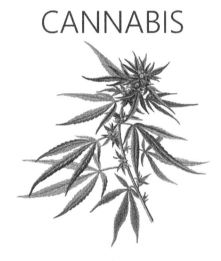

| *"A weed is a plant whose virtue is not yet known." ~Ralph Waldo Emerson*

Cannabis is derived from the cannabis sativa plant. Used by ancient civilizations for Tantric rituals and spiritual meditation, cannabis essential oil's therapeutic aroma enhances emotional and mental well-being by releasing stress and relaxing the body while lifting the spirit. Cannabis contain high amounts of a substance commonly referred to as THC - or tetrahydrocannabinol - which is well known for its psychotropic abilities. This oil treats a wide range of illnesses including cancer, anorexia, pain, and inflammation. Improves the quality of sleep, boosts appetite, optimizes digestion, reduces pain, and protects heart health.

There is much more to learn about the healing qualities of this oil. It has also been used for a number of neurodegenerative disorders such as Alzheimer's disease,

Parkinson's and Tourette's syndrome. Cannabis and hemp oil come from the same species – cannabis sativa. Hemp oil, however, is quite different to cannabis oil. Hemp is commonly used for topical ointments, fiber and paper.

Cannabis treatments are effective in reducing anxiety in those suffering from PTSD.

Blends well with; Eucalyptus bergamot, lemon, lime, orange, and lavender essential oil.

Beauty: Add a couple of drops of cannabis to a carrier oil to promote a healthy-looking skin. When applied topically, cannabis oil stimulates the shedding of dead skin cells and promotes the growth of new ones. Add a few drops to your bath water for a relaxing bath at the end of the day.

Health: Cannabis oil slows the signs of aging and reduces skin spots due to its natural antioxidants that fight against cellular damage caused by free radicals. Cannabis essential oil is an effective treatment method for psoriasis and eczema.

Tests have shown the ability of cannabis oil to treat eye conditions such as glaucoma and macular degeneration. Glaucoma is a serious optic nerve disease that can lead to blindness. So not apply cannabis essential oil directly to the eye, but rather through aromatherapy.

Lifestyle and Diet Changes:

When using cannabis oil treatment for cancer, steps must be taken in changing your diet, and lifestyle. Studies show that cancer cannot sustain in an alkaline body. You will need to eat an alkaline diet comprising of lots of organic greens every day. Plant protein fights the growth of cancer. Start drinking as many raw fruits and vegetable smoothies as much as possible. You may like to check out the next book in the series, "Little Book Of Smoothies," for some great blending ideas.

Eat little to no meat or dairy products, the proteins in these foods will promote cancer growth. You should also stop eating sugar. Replace the use of sugar with natural alternative like dates or raw honey.

Let us hope that further studies will continue to prove the health benefits derived from cannabis oil – which in most cases, is a healthier alternative to the side effects of pharmaceutical drugs.

This is like the Holy Grail of cancer medicine; vitamin D produced a drop in cancer rates greater than that for quitting smoking, or indeed any other countermeasure in existence. ~ Dennis Mangan, clinical laboratory scientist.

JOT DOWN YOUR OWN OIL BLENDS.

PATTI ROBERTS

PATTI ROBERTS

PATTI ROBERTS

NOTES

SAMPLE FROM LITTLE BOOK OF SMOOTHIES.

TROPICAL TREAT

Serves 2
1 frozen banana
½ an orange
½ cup pineapple
1 tbsp of spirulina
1 cup coconut water
½ cup water
Handful of ice cubes

Pineapple is a good snack for those about to take a long flight, and others at risk for blood clots.

INFO ABOUT BANANAS.

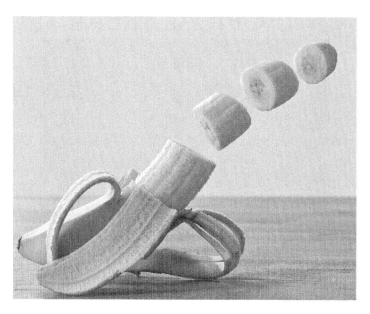

- Eating bananas help prevent asthma, cancer, high blood pressure, diabetes, cardiovascular disease, and digestive problems.
- Bananas are rich in potassium and fiber.
- Ripen bananas at room temperature – they are perfect to eat when they have black spots on the skin.
- The warmer the temperature, the faster bananas will ripen. To slow ripening, bananas should be refrigerated.
- To ripen faster, place the banana in a brown paper bag at room temperature.
- The potassium in bananas may reduce the risk of kidney stones forming as people age.
- Ripe mashed bananas can be used in baked goods to replace oil or butter.

BANANA ORANGE GINGER ZINGER

Serves 2
1 ½ cups of coconut water
1 banana sliced (frozen is nice)
¾ cup vanilla yogurt
½ an orange
1 radish
1 tsp honey
1 level tsp freshly grated ginger – organic is best.

The potassium in bananas may reduce the risk of kidney stones forming as people age.

Info About Pineapples

- Pineapples contain bromelain, an enzyme which can break down protein. Bromelain is a powerful anti-inflammatory, which can provide relief to those suffering inflammatory diseases like arthritis. Bromelain is a complex mixture of substances which is extracted from the stem and core of the pineapple.

- You can cut off the top of the pineapple (leaves) to grow a new plant. Pineapples take about 18-20 months before they are ready to harvest. Pineapples ripen faster upside down. Each pineapple scale is an individual berry.

- Pineapples contain manganese, which may be helpful in preventing osteoporosis in post-menopausal women.

- Due in part to its high amount of vitamin C and antioxidants, pineapples can help reduce the risk of macular degeneration, a disease that affects your eyes as you age. Eating 3 or more servings of fruit per day may lower your risk of age-related macular degeneration, the primary cause of vision loss in older adults.

PINEAPPLE CONCOCTION

Serves 2
1 cup pineapple chunks (include the stem)
½ cup of cucumber
1 ½ cups coconut water
1 carrot
1 tbsp of pumpkin seeds (pepitas)
2 tbsp of chia seeds
A piece of ginger
Handful of ice cubes

Coconut water is a good source of magnesium, which studies have shown to improve insulin sensitivity and decrease blood sugar levels in people with type 2 diabetes and prediabetes.

I hope you have enjoyed reading this edition of the Witchwood Estate Collectables Ebook featuring the benefits of using essential oils in and around your home and office. If you have, please leave a short review to help others find the book.

Make sure you join my newsletter and be kept up to date on new releases, special promotions, and freebies.

JOIN UP FOR PATTI ROBERTS NEWSLETTER:
http://bit.ly/PattiRobertsNewsletter

CONTACT PATTI ROBERTS.

Twitter: http://bit.ly/1szIGfI
Facebook: http://on.fb.me/1waO1jO
Goodreads: http://bit.ly/1tdwu8f

ABOUT THE AUTHOR.

PATTI ROBERTS was born in Brisbane Australia but soon moved to Darwin in the Northern Territory. Her son Luke was born in 1980. Her son and two grandsons are the three leading men in Patti's life. She currently lives in Cairns, Queensland, where she is writing the Paradox Series of books. Since then, Patti has commenced writing the Witchwood Estate series, and a contemporary romance, About Three Authors – Whoever Said Love Was Easy? Patti has also published a non-fiction book, Surviving Tracy, featuring true stories from survivors of Cyclone Tracy which devastated Darwin in the Northern Territory in 1974.

Patti's books are available worldwide from, libraries, bookstores on request, and all the better online stores.

Going vegan in 2019, Patti is committed to saving the animals, the planet, and the host of rewarding health benefits.

Made in the USA
Monee, IL
05 August 2020